WINDS AND WEATHER

Written and illustrated by

JOHN KAUFMANN

WORLD'S WORK LTD

The Windmill Press

Kingswood Tadworth Surrey

By the Same Author

Birds in Flight

For Howard Selsam, who loved the winds.

Grateful acknowledgment is given
to Mr. Bert Weiner, for reading and
criticizing this manuscript.

Copyright © 1971 by John Kaufmann
First published in Great Britain 1973 by
World's Work Ltd, The Windmill Press, Kingswood, Tadworth, Surrey
Printed in Great Britain by
Fletcher & Son Ltd, Norwich

SBN 437 52121 4

Contents

When the Wind Blows

The wind is blowing. Falling leaves scatter and swirl away. Children hold tugging strings as their kites lift aloft. Dirty smoke from cars, trucks, and chimneys drifts swiftly upward and disappears. Silent boats with puffed-out sails tilt over and drive hard across the bay. Ripe seed pods break, sending out fluffy, white parachutes. They ride up on the wind and land in distant places where they root. Big birds and tiny insects coast downwind for many miles. In flat farm country windwheels generate electricity and pump water. In faraway lands windmills grind the grain. Out in the desert, windblown sand slowly builds or wears away the dunes. High above the sea, a jet airliner streaks eastward, boosted along by a great current of the upper air.

All these things happen because the wind blows. Without any wind the air is still. Wind moves across the earth, making kites, smoke, yachts, and many other things move too. However, wind does not exist as something separate from the rest of nature. It is the carrier of all weather. Winds blow hot or cold, humid or dry, from different directions at varying speeds. If you learn to recognize the various winds, you often can predict what the weather will be.

The daily weather is caused by moving cells of high-pressure or low-pressure air. These areas may extend hundreds and even thousands of miles. A simple way to think of high- and low-pressure air is that more air is present in a certain space under high pressure. Conversely, less air is contained in the same space when the pressure is low. When an area of high pressure is next to one of lower pressure, air always moves from the high towards the low. You can make a simple test of this fact by blowing up a balloon. When you force extra air

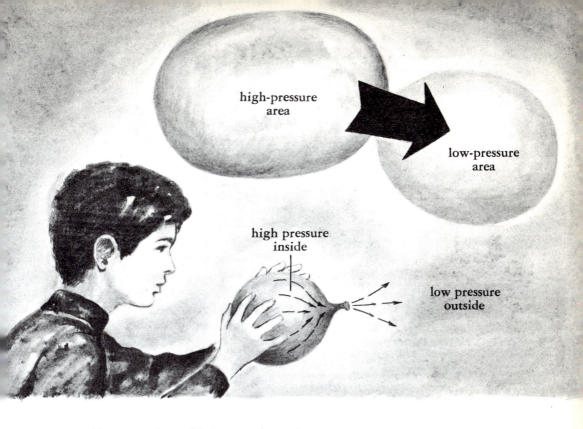

high-pressure
area

low-pressure
area

high pressure
inside

low pressure
outside

Air moves from high pressure to low pressure.

inside the balloon, you raise the pressure. If you
relax your grip on the nozzle, the high-pressure air
inside rushes out towards the lower-pressure air surrounding the balloon. This movement of air from
high to low pressure is a basic law of meteorology,
the science of weather study.

Wind Instruments

Before you can study the wind, you have to know the size, shape, and pressure of the air cells that cause it. They determine from what direction, how fast, and for how long a certain wind will blow. Air pressure is measured by an instrument called the "barometer." A glass tube with a vacuum, or zero air pressure, at the closed top end is filled with a liquid metal called mercury. The lower end is bent up and open to the pressure of the outside air. As the air pressure outside increases, it raises

Barometers measure air pressure.

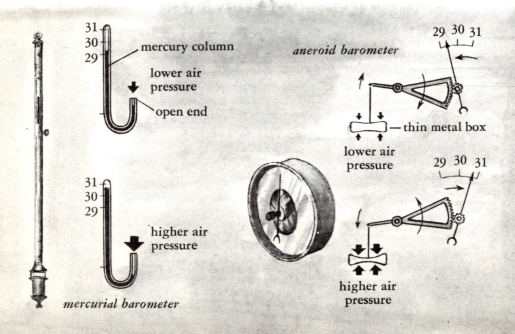

mercury column

lower air pressure

open end

higher air pressure

mercurial barometer

aneroid barometer

29 30 31

— thin metal box

lower air pressure

29 30 31

higher air pressure

the column inside the tube. When the outside air pressure decreases, there is less push on the mercury, so it sinks in the tube. The tube is marked in millibars or inches. When the weather report says, for example, that the barometer is 30.01 and falling, it means that the mercury column measures 30.01 inches high and is going lower. The aneroid barometer is a type that many people have at home. Its thin metal box contracts when outside air pressure rises and expands when the pressure falls. This movement turns a needle across a dial marked in millibars or inches of mercury.

Meteorologists, who study and forecast the weather, make up the weather maps you see in your newspaper and on television. On these maps they mark air-pressure readings taken all over the country and at sea. Lines of air pressure, called "isobars," are drawn to locate the high- and low-pressure cells. These cells and their accompanying winds are often called "systems." At any point along an isobar the air pressure is the same.

Isobars close together indicate strong winds.

Isobars far apart indicate lighter winds.

isobars and wind flow

Where isobars are closest together, there are the biggest changes in air pressure and the strongest winds. The pattern of the isobars shows both the general direction and the comparative speed of the wind in any part of the country.

However, there are more direct and precise ways to find out wind direction and speed. The wind vane, or its popular version the weather vane, indicates wind direction. A wind vane is a pivoting stick with a large side area on one end. That end acts like a rudder. It always swings downwind and steadies itself in line with the wind flow. The pointer on the other end shows where the wind is coming from. Wind direction is given as the compass direction from which it blows, for example, north or northwest. Sailors use a more exact direction, for instance, south southwest or east northeast.

The most accurate directions are given in compass degrees. On a compass east is 90 degrees, south is 180 degrees, west is 270 degrees, and north is 360 degrees. For precise navigation, such as that used in aviation, wind direction is located by the exact degree.

The wind vane shows wind direction.

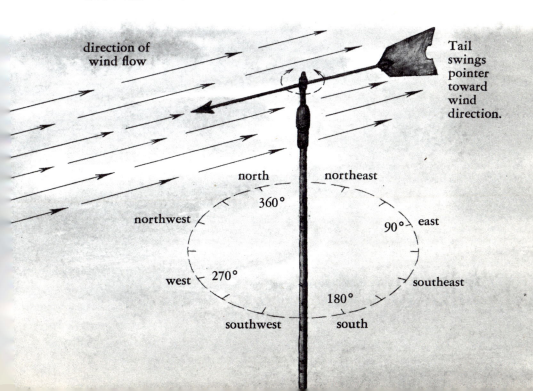

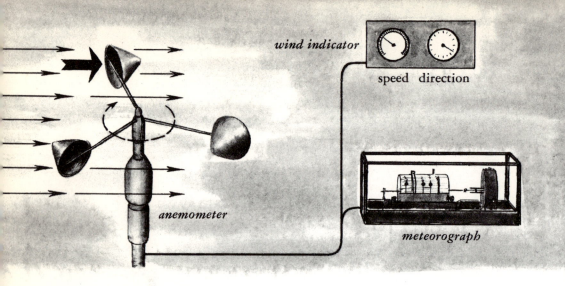

wind indicator

speed direction

anemometer

meteorograph

The anemometer measures wind speed.

Wind speed is measured by an instrument called the "anemometer." It consists of three or four cups attached to the outer ends of arms rotating on a centre shaft. The wind pushes the cups and spins the shaft. As the shaft spins, a dial in the weather station indicates the speed of the wind in miles per hour. Both wind direction and speed are recorded continually on graph paper by an instrument called the "meteorograph," to which the wind vane and anemometer are connected electrically.

In the early days of sailing there were no precise wind instruments. Still sailors needed to know how fast the wind was blowing in order to set the right amount of sail. In 1805 Admiral Francis Beaufort of the Royal Navy made up a scale of wind speeds according to their effects upon a frigate's sails. Here is a modified Beaufort scale showing the ranges of wind speed and their effects upon land.

The Beaufort Wind Scale

Beaufort Number	Miles Per Hour	Description	Effect
0	0-1	calm	smoke rises vertically
1	1-3	light air	smoke drifts slowly
2	4-7	slight breeze	leaves rustle
3	8-12	gentle breeze	leaves and twigs in motion
4	13-18	moderate breeze	small branches move
5	19-24	fresh breeze	small trees sway
6	25-31	strong breeze	large branches sway
7	32-38	moderate gale	whole trees in motion
8	39-46	fresh gale	twigs break off trees
9	47-54	strong gale	branches break
10	55-63	whole gale	trees snap and are blown down
11	64-72	storm	widespread damage
12	73-82	hurricane	extreme damage

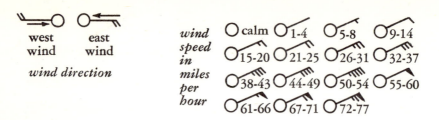

west wind | east wind

wind direction

wind speed in miles per hour

O calm	O 1-4	O 5-8	O 9-14
O 15-20	O 21-25	O 26-31	O 32-37
O 38-43	O 44-49	O 50-54	O 55-60
O 61-66	O 67-71	O 72-77	

Beaufort wind symbols used on weather maps

Symbols based on the Beaufort scale, showing wind direction and speed, are used on weather maps today. A tail pointing towards a circle shows wind direction. The speed is shown by the number of markings added to the tail. The greater the speed, the greater the number of markings.

means of checking high-altitude winds

aircraft

balloons

rockets

Winds at higher altitudes are different from surface winds, and meteorologists need to know about them too. They check these winds with instrument-carrying balloons released from the ground. The balloons rise up, drift with the wind, and radio back data to weather stations. Sometimes radar also is used to follow their path as they ascend. Special aircraft and instrument-carrying rockets study the winds at very high altitudes.

The Great Circulation System

Surface winds are only a part of a much greater movement of air that takes place far above the ground and around the globe. You probably have seen photographs taken by the astronauts. They show the globe covered by swirling cloud patterns, stretching and curving across continents and oceans. Half the world's weather is spread out in one picture. All winds, from a giant hurricane to the slightest breeze, are part of that great whirl. Each

the earth's circulation system seen from space

movement of air, great or small, is an interlocking
part of the weather in a certain place within a large
region, which in turn fits into a worldwide pattern.
All the different winds work together like parts of
an immense circulation system and move the ocean
of air, the atmosphere, that surrounds our planet.

16

The atmosphere is made up of four main layers: the troposphere, the stratosphere, the ionosphere, and the exosphere. Only the two lower layers, however—the troposphere and the stratosphere—are important to meteorologists. All weather as we know it takes place within the troposphere. Winds blow over land and sea, clouds move, rain and snow fall. On top of the troposphere is a dividing level called the tropopause. Vast, powerful movements of air occur there and help drive the atmosphere. Above the tropopause, the clear and largely calm stratosphere extends its thinner and thinner air

layers of the atmosphere

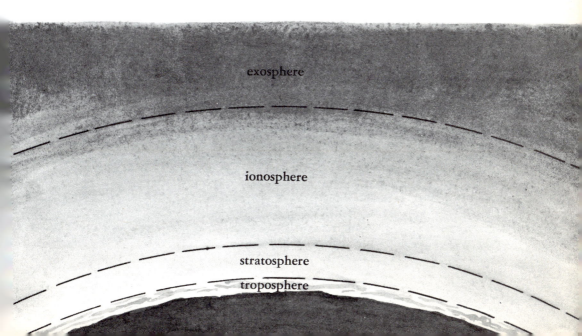

exosphere

ionosphere

stratosphere

troposphere

outward to about fifty miles. Although winds of over 200 miles per hour sometimes blow there, jet pilots prefer to fly in the smooth stratosphere rather than in the ever-changing troposphere.

The countless tons of atmosphere enveloping the earth are moved by energy from the sun. The sun's rays heat the lands and oceans. They, in turn, heat great masses of surface air, which expand and rise, setting the atmosphere in motion.

The sun's heat energy moves from the equator to the poles.

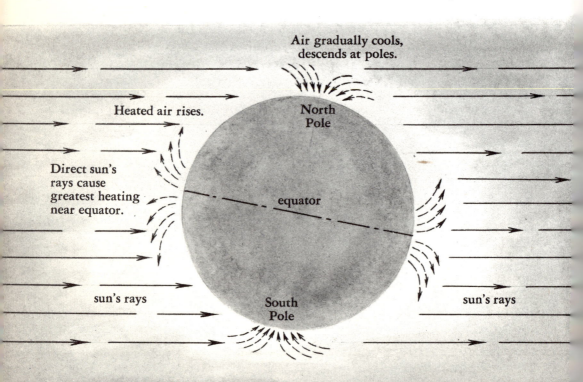

Most of the sun's radiant energy is absorbed by tropical regions near the equator. Throughout the year the sun's rays strike that portion of the globe more directly than any other. North and south of the tropics the sun shines from lower angles and gives less heat. At the poles, where the sun shines at very shallow angles, little heat is absorbed. Yet the tropics do not get hotter and hotter, and the polar regions do not get colder and colder. Instead, they both show a steady range of temperatures from year to year.

In order to keep this temperature balance, there is a constant transfer of heated air from the tropics to the colder parts of the globe. Hot air rises from the tropics and cools as it moves north and south over colder regions. Eventually it loses all its heat and sinks down at the poles. Scientists do not understand fully how the heated tropical air travels. They do know, however, that its movement is not a direct and simple flow between the equator and the poles.

Coriolis Force

Recent studies show that upper level winds, for example those at 40,000 feet, move from west to east in every region except the tropics. This wind direction might seem to contradict the idea of a northward flow of upper air in the northern hemisphere. However, an important force acts upon all

how Coriolis force turns the winds

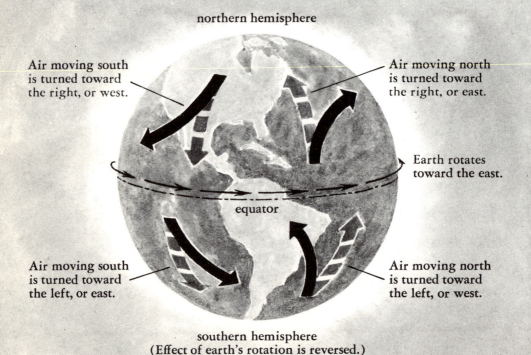

northern hemisphere

Air moving south is turned toward the right, or west.

Air moving north is turned toward the right, or east.

Earth rotates toward the east.

equator

Air moving south is turned toward the left, or east.

Air moving north is turned toward the left, or west.

southern hemisphere
(Effect of earth's rotation is reversed.)

moving air, turning it away from its original direction. It is called the Coriolis force.

As air moves across the earth, it travels across a surface that is also moving. The earth's surface moves eastward, due to the planet's rotation on its axis. Thus, earth moves out from under a wind, changing the wind's path across its surface. If air is moving north in the northern hemisphere, the earth's rotation and the Coriolis force it produces causes the air to turn towards the east, or the right. If air is moving south in the northern hemisphere, Coriolis force turns it towards the west, again to the right. Below the equator the effect is reversed, and the Coriolis force sends winds to the left.

Scientists believe that swirling disturbances of the upper atmosphere temporarily change the eastward flow of air in the northern hemisphere and carry it towards the North Pole. In this way warm air from the tropical and temperate zones meets cold polar air at high altitudes along the polar front. This front circles the North Pole, giving

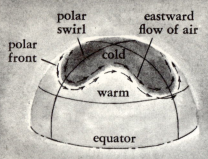

polar swirl
eastward flow of air
polar front
cold
warm
equator

Polar front bulges and swells.

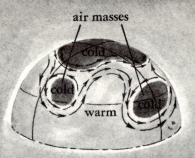

air masses
cold
cold
cold
warm

Areas of cold air break off
as separate air masses.

how cold air masses form at the polar front

the world a cap of cold air called the polar swirl. At the polar front, the huge regions of warm and cold air struggle against each other like two invisible armies of the atmosphere. The polar swirl undulates, bulges, and swells, until one or more areas of cold air break off. Then they move south as separate air masses, crossing the continents and helping to shape the weather patterns of the hemisphere.

22

Jet Streams

Until recently scientists thought that the tropopause formed an unbroken, horizontal layer on top
of the troposphere. However, research has shown
that it is divided into sections with different altitude
levels that overlap each other. The sections are
known as the tropical, extratropical, and arctic tropopauses. Along the breaks between them are
found the famous jet streams, great rivers of wind
that move at much swifter speeds than the normal
flow of the upper air.

overlapping layers of the tropopause

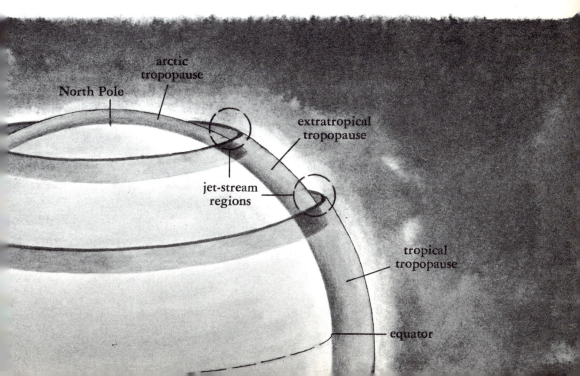

In the northern hemisphere the most important break occurs at the polar front. There the extra-tropical and the arctic tropopauses overlap. Some-times the difference in altitude between them is more than 30,000 feet. The difference in tempera-ture is equally great. Both factors help to create one of the world's most important winds, the polar jet stream.

Much of the energy that moves the atmosphere is centred within the polar jet stream. Like all jet streams, it blows generally towards the east, since it is part of the overall movement of the upper air. It is shaped like a flattened tube from three to five hundred miles wide, and from a few thou-sand feet to as much as three or four miles thick. The centre core contains the strongest winds, as high as 100 to 200 miles per hour in winter over the northern Atlantic and the British Isles and up to 300 miles per hour over the western Pacific.

Sometimes the polar jet runs unbroken com-pletely around the world, but usually it is separated

jet-stream paths

northern hemisphere

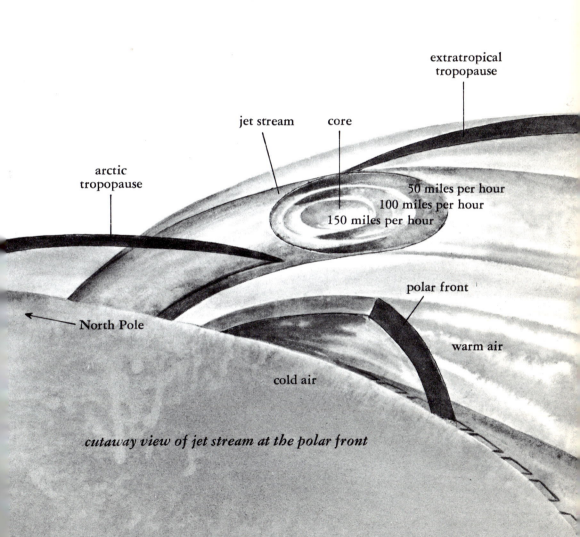

extratropical
tropopause

jet stream   core

arctic
tropopause

50 miles per hour
100 miles per hour
150 miles per hour

polar front

← North Pole

warm air

cold air

cutaway view of jet stream at the polar front

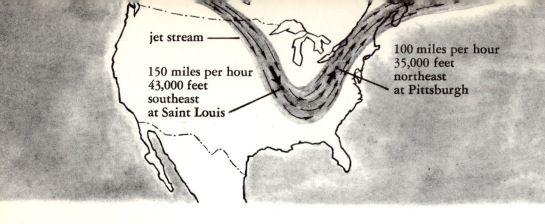

Jet streams vary in speed, altitude, and direction.

into two or more parts that follow the shape of the polar front. Breaks and snaking movements change the jet's direction, top speed, and altitude at different locations. For instance, over Saint Louis in the U.S.A. it may travel southeast at 150 miles per hour at 43,000 feet, while over Pittsburgh, it may run northeast at 100 miles per hour at 35,000 feet. These meandering streams strongly affect the weather, because they usually steer large storm systems located beneath them.

Today scientists are devoting much study to jet streams and other movements of the upper air. They want to know just how the heated tropical

26

air is carried to the polar regions and how its heat energy helps to move the tremendous mass of the atmosphere around the earth.

Prevailing Wind Zones

As great masses of air move from the tropics to the poles, air rises from the earth in some regions and sinks in others. Where an abundance of air settles earthward and perhaps merges with other masses of surface air, high-pressure zones or anti-cyclones are created. Where air rises from the surface or flows away, it leaves behind zones of low pressure.

how zones of high and low pressure form

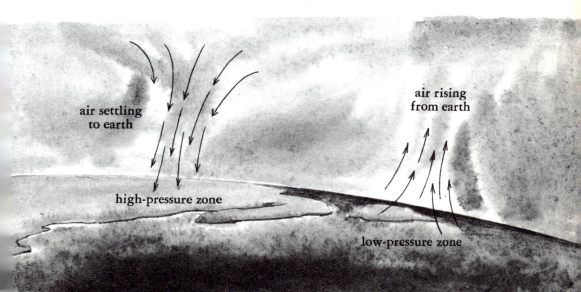

air settling to earth

air rising from earth

high-pressure zone

low-pressure zone

High-pressure air flows outward from its centre towards surrounding regions of lower pressure. Coriolis force affects the movement of this air. It turns a northward-moving current towards the east, and then the outward flow circles south, revolving around the centre of the system. A southward moving current turns towards the west, and then circles north. Thus, the air mass as a whole spirals in a clockwise direction.

Air in a high flows outward and clockwise.

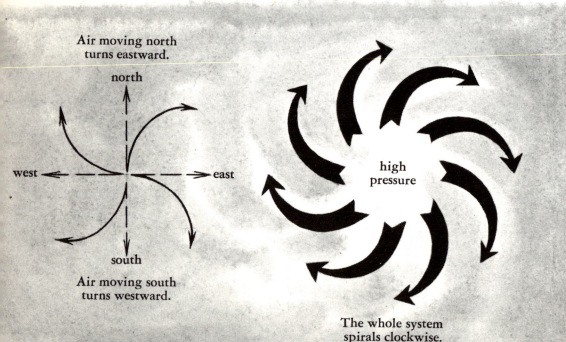

Air moving north turns eastward.

north

west

east

south

Air moving south turns westward.

high pressure

The whole system spirals clockwise.

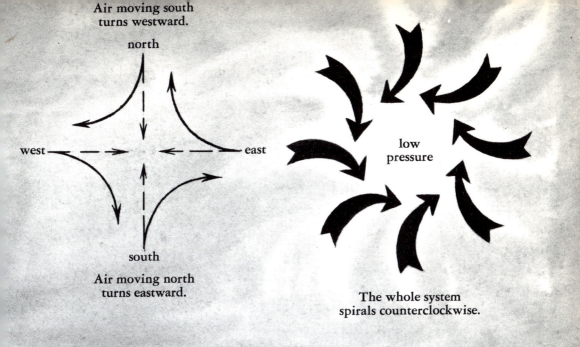

Air moving south turns westward.

north

west — — — east

south

Air moving north turns eastward.

low pressure

The whole system spirals counterclockwise.

Air in a low flows inward and counterclockwise.

A low-pressure system or depression works in just the opposite way. Air flows from surrounding regions of high pressure inward towards the centre of a low. Coriolis force turns a northward-moving current towards the east as before, but the inward flow of air causes it to circle the low and spiral in a counterclockwise direction.

29

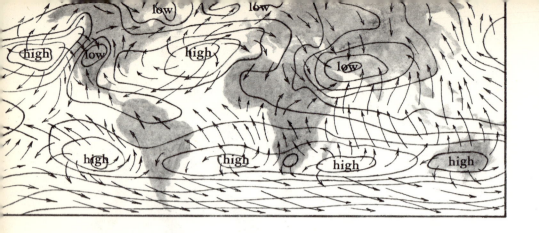

prevailing highs and lows of world wind zones in July

High- and low-pressure regions form the world's prevailing wind zones. Scientists map these zones on the basis of information gathered at weather stations around the world. Because they are closely linked to the overall circulation, many of the zones and their winds show little change during much of the year. However, changes in weather and passing storms can cause temporary wind shifts for a day or more within all prevailing wind zones.

One important wind zone is located near the equator. When heated air rises from tropical seas, it leaves behind low-pressure zones that extend around the world. In the centre of a low there is no pressure difference to create winds, so the equatorial oceans are often without the slightest breeze. Sailing ships of old avoided these areas of calm, or doldrums, whenever possible.

Another large region of prevailing winds is found north of the doldrums. Air flowing clockwise from the Hawaiian high of the Pacific Ocean

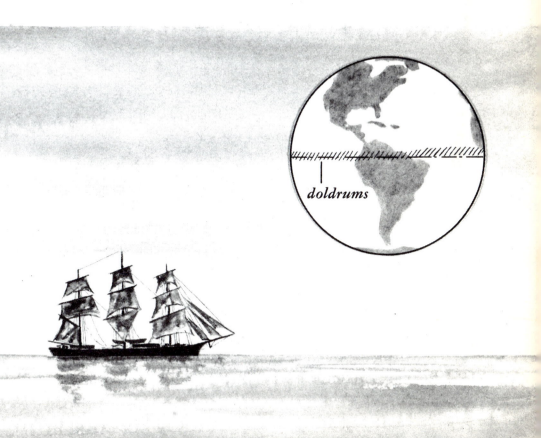

doldrums

and the Azores high of the Atlantic Ocean moves south towards the low-pressure areas near the equator. This air is turned westward by Coriolis force to produce the northeast trade winds. The two great highs persist throughout the year, and so do the prevailing winds they produce. In the old days, Columbus and other sea voyagers took advantage of the northeast trade winds by sailing in a southerly direction from Europe to the Americas.

In the centre of highs, as well as in lows, winds are light and often calm. Wide areas of persistent

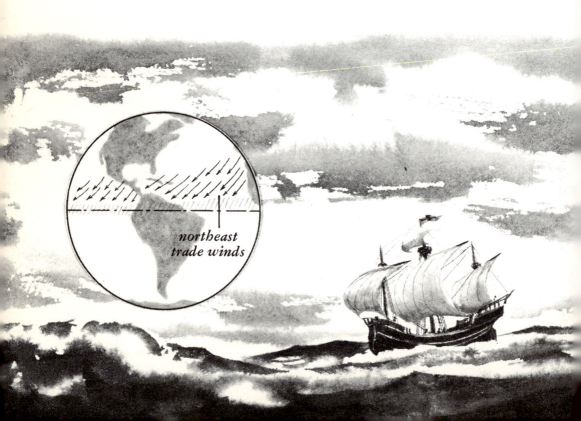

northeast trade winds

horse latitudes

calm are found at about thirty degrees north latitude, where both the Azores and Hawaiian highs are centred. Spanish ships carrying horses to the New World colonies were often becalmed in the Atlantic Ocean for long periods. When the horses had used up their share of feed and water and were starving to death, they were thrown overboard to lighten the load so the ships could get moving again. These poor beasts gave the regions their name—the horse latitudes.

Surface air moves northward from the high-pressure zones of the horse latitudes. Coriolis force turns this flow eastward, forming the winds called the prevailing westerlies, which are the dominant ones over Great Britain and the United States. These prevailing surface winds, added to the eastward movement of the upper air and the jet streams, carry our weather in a general west to east direction.

Still farther north, in the Bering Sea and the southern Arctic Ocean, winds blow mainly from the east. Cold air sinks at the poles, moves south, and is deflected westward by Coriolis force. This pattern causes the cold winds known as the polar easterlies.

prevailing westerlies

polar easterlies

Below the equator, similar wind zones exist. One of them corresponds to the prevailing westerlies in the northern hemisphere. Between forty and sixty degrees south latitude west winds blow at high speed around the world, blocked at only one place by the southern tip of South America. This world-wide belt of winds is the most persistent as well as the largest of the prevailing wind zones. Except for temporary storm disruptions, the wind blows all year round from the same direction. Storms are frequent there, and in the great days of sailing they earned the region its name, the roaring forties.

roaring forties

American clipper ships homeward bound from the Orient filled their sails with these pushing gales to make record-breaking speed runs across the Pacific Ocean.

The greatest force acting to shift the prevailing wind zones during the year is the uneven, changing heating of the earth by the sun. The earth tilts on its axis as it moves around the sun, so that it is not heated equally during the year. First the northern, then the southern hemisphere, receives the greater amount of heat. This seasonal change affects the overall circulation of the atmosphere and, in turn, causes the prevailing wind zones to move.

The best example of seasonal change in a prevailing wind is found along the shores of the Indian Ocean and the Arabian Sea. There the famous monsoon blows across India, Burma, and East Asia. In summer, warm air rises from the low-pressure area over the land, causing high-pressure air to flow in from the sea. The constant onshore winds carry lots of moisture, which falls day after

Changing heat of the sun causes prevailing wind zones to move.

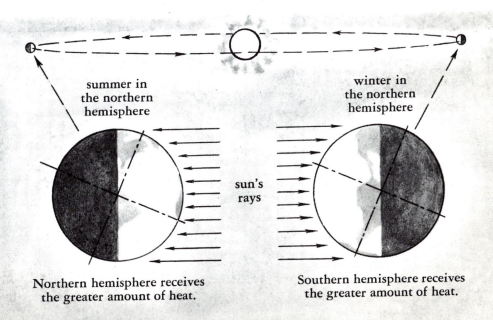

summer in
the northern
hemisphere

winter in
the northern
hemisphere

sun's
rays

Northern hemisphere receives
the greater amount of heat.

Southern hemisphere receives
the greater amount of heat.

In winter, monsoon winds blow offshore.

In summer, monsoon winds blow onshore.

day as rain. In winter, the land is cooler and the air over it has higher pressure than that over the ocean. Accordingly, the winds reverse and blow steadily offshore. The regularity of the monsoon permits the growing of rice and other crops that need a wet season before planting and a dry season for growing and harvesting. Lesser forms of the monsoon, though not so named, are found along the Gulf Coast of the United States, the northern coast of Brazil, and the west coast of Africa.

Daily Winds

Prevailing winds are created by pressure zones that may not move for long periods of time. Daily winds, on the other hand, are caused mainly by air masses that can travel hundreds of miles across country in a day. Both kinds of wind depend upon the flow of air from high to low pressure.

Highs are like invisible mountains with low-pressure troughs, or valleys, in between. Air moves out and down from the peak of a high, its centre of pressure. Coriolis force turns this flow clockwise in the northern hemisphere. Low-pressure air

mountains (highs) and valleys (lows) of air pressure

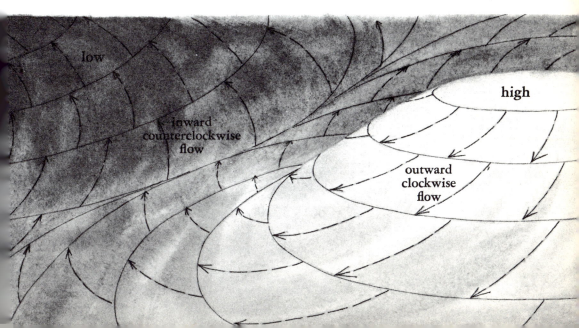

flows inward, and Coriolis force turns it counter-clockwise. However, another force called surface friction also affects wind direction, depending upon the altitude.

Air moving close to the surface, below 2000 feet, does not flow as freely as air higher up because of greater friction between it and the ground. Gravity pulls the atmosphere downward and exerts the greatest pressure upon the lowest layer of air. Thus, this lowest layer is slowed down and its flow is disrupted, because it directly contacts the surface. The

Wind direction varies at different altitudes.

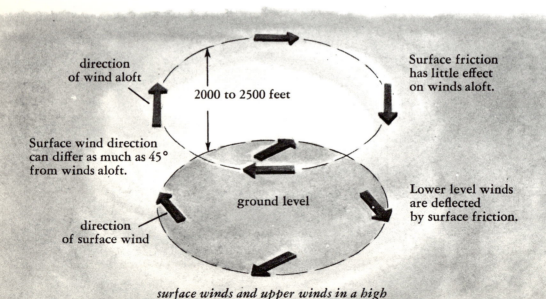

direction of wind aloft

2000 to 2500 feet

Surface friction has little effect on winds aloft.

Surface wind direction can differ as much as 45° from winds aloft.

ground level

Lower level winds are deflected by surface friction.

direction of surface wind

surface winds and upper winds in a high

next higher layer is slowed and disrupted less, and the next still less.

At about 2000 to 2500 feet above the ground there is little surface friction. The wind direction is controlled entirely by Coriolis force and follows the lines of the isobars that outline the air mass. Down lower, however, the air drags across the terrain and resists the Coriolis force, so the winds blow at an angle across the isobars. For this reason there is a difference of about forty-five degrees between wind direction at ground level and its direction at 2000 feet and higher. Aviation meteorologists take this difference into account. When reporting winds aloft, they give wind directions and speeds for various altitudes.

Because upper winds are less exposed to surface friction, they blow faster, smoother, and more steadily than lower winds. As a result, the jet streams and the upper air patterns in general show little resemblance to the separated shapes of air masses near the ground.

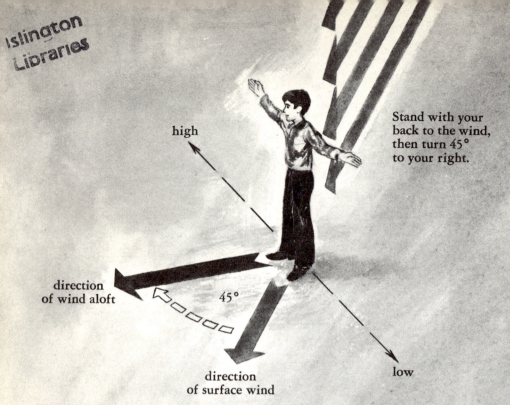

Stand with your
back to the wind,
then turn 45°
to your right.

direction
of wind aloft

45°

direction
of surface wind

low

locating highs and lows by wind direction

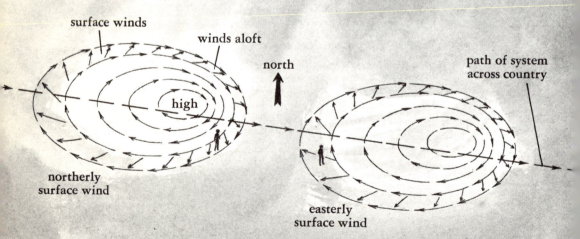

surface winds

winds aloft

north

path of system
across country

high

northerly
surface wind

easterly
surface wind

*Wind direction depends upon your location
within a passing high or low.*

winds of highs and lows

As highs and lows pass the area where you live, the winds change direction. By following a simple procedure, you can estimate roughly where the highs and lows are centred. Since highs usually bring good weather and lows bad weather, you can judge what sort is coming your way. First, stand with your back to the wind. Then turn about forty-five degrees to your right, to allow for the effect on wind direction caused by surface friction. Now your back is to the wind direction aloft. According to a well-established formula, called the Buys Ballot's law, you can assume that the high is to your right and the low is to your left.

If the high is somewhere to the west, for example southwest towards the Azores, fair weather is probably moving closer to you with the prevailing westerlies. As the high comes closer and passes by, the surface winds will change their direction and speed, depending upon your position within the clockwise spiral.

When two highs of different temperature,

humidity, and wind flow come together, a front may form between them. The advance line of a front is marked by a low-pressure trough caused by the edge of the warmer air mass rising as the cooler air mass wedges underneath. In a cold front the colder air mass pushes back the warmer one. In a warm front the warmer air mass overrides the colder one and pushes it away. In either case, the rising, warm air cools, condenses, forms clouds, and often falls as rain or snow.

winds of cold fronts and warm fronts

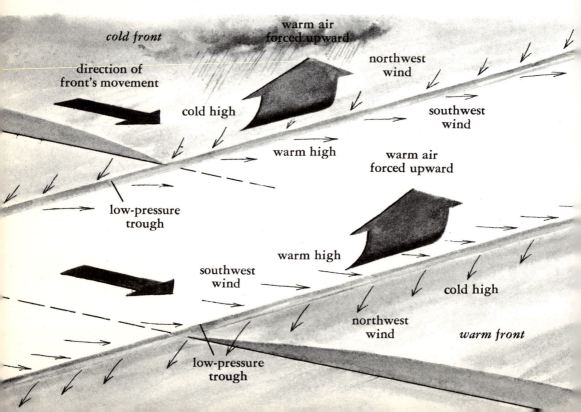

Fronts may travel very fast and bring rapid weather changes on strong winds. You may have noticed the sudden arrival of a cold front in summer. At first the air is still and heavy with humidity. Then a breeze springs up as skies grow dark. A shower or even a thunderstorm occurs as the advance line of the front passes. Soon the wind starts gusting hard from between north and west, bending trees and making clouds fly. After a while the air is much cooler and the sun sparkles in a clear blue sky. In winter, such invasions of cold air can drop the temperature quickly well below freezing, and in northern areas it may fall far below zero. Warm fronts, on the other hand, can push the thermometer up just as rapidly to a very high temperature.

Cold winds from invading highs are familiar in many countries. In Mexico and Central America the Tehuantepecer blows from the north when polar air breaks through and thrusts far south. The Texas norther appears when cold fronts penetrate south into the Great Plains. A strong norther can drop temperatures from the mid seventies or eighties to below freezing in only a half a day.

Tehuantepecer

northeaster

Below the equator, cold air comes out of high-pressure areas in the polar regions of Antarctica. The "southerly busters" of Australia bring storms and cold. However, the warmer ocean surrounding Australia lessens their effect, so the busters seldom lower temperatures more than twenty or thirty degrees.

The winter northeaster of the American New England states is somewhat different. Its slightly warmer, humid air raises temperatures fifteen to twenty degrees. It blows from the northeast when polar Atlantic air, heavily laden with ocean

47

moisture, replaces dry polar Canadian air. However, the slight temperature rise seldom brings much comfort, since northeasters have buried New England under its worst blizzards.

Winds carrying warm air masses are also familiar to people in many lands. In Palestine and Syria the well-known sirocco blows hot, dry, dusty air from the deserts of Arabia. Southerly winds, also called sirocco come to Spain, southern France, Sicily, Yugoslavia and Greece from the African deserts. However, scientists call them modified

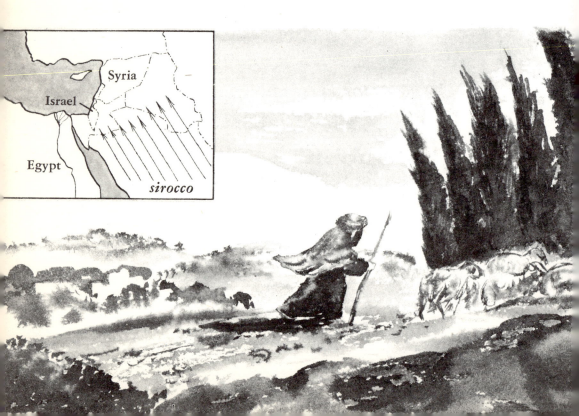

sirocco, since they cool somewhat and pick up moisture as they pass over the Mediterranean Sea. This sirocco blows mostly in the winter, when its warmth is welcome.

The harmattan is a dry, northeast wind blowing from the Sahara Desert over the west coast of Africa. Although it brings sunny skies, the great amount of dust it carries obscures visibility for hundreds of miles out into the Atlantic Ocean.

These winds flow with little interruption across the earth's surface. They are not changed to any great extent by the shape of the terrain over which they blow. Other important winds, however, are strongly affected by the land underneath them.

High mountains are the greatest obstacles to air flowing across the earth. Their height, shape, and rough surfaces all have an effect on the wind. Deep valleys near high mountains increase the amount of altitude change. As altitude increases, temperatures fall. Thus, when winds crossing mountains are forced upward, the air within them cools. When

Moisture forms clouds.

Rising air cools and condenses.

Dry descending air heats up rapidly.

how foehn winds are formed

cooling occurs, the water vapour in the air often condenses into tiny droplets and forms clouds above the mountains. With much of its moisture removed, the wind going down the other side is drier. As it descends it warms up rapidly.

Dry, hot winds blowing down from mountains are called foehn (pronounced like *fern* without the *r*) winds. The word comes from a mountain wind in the Swiss and German Alps. The discomfort caused by the foehn in Europe has been linked to sickness and mental depression, as well as a rise in the number of suicides.

50

The dense clouds that form as moisture condenses above mountain peaks are called the foehn
wall. On the downwind side of the mountain the
wind rebounds in waves that extend for miles.
Foehn waves often form lens-shaped clouds. Glider
pilots watch for these clouds and use the swiftly
rising wind currents that they indicate to reach
great heights. In 1964, Paul Bickle, an American
pilot, soared to a record 46,267 feet on the
foehn wave of the Sierra Nevada Mountains in

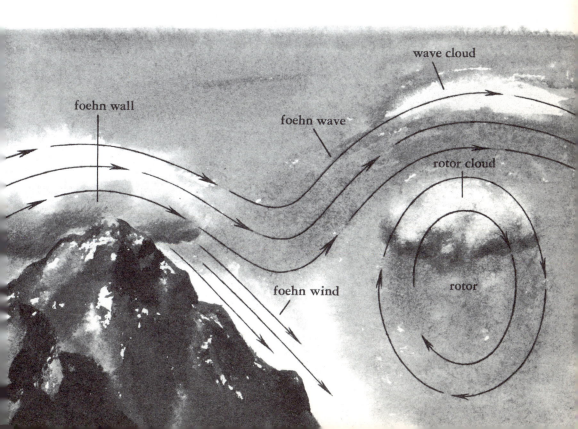

wave cloud

foehn wall

foehn wave

rotor cloud

foehn wind

rotor

California. Foehn currents also create severe turbulence, called a "rotor," over the downwind slopes. Another glider pilot was caught in a foehn rotor and lost consciousness when his craft was ripped away from him. When he came to he was falling, luckily with his parachute still intact. All that remained of the glider were the rudder controls, still hanging from his feet.

A foehn wind named the chinook blows from the Rocky Mountains down across the Great Plains in winter. Its hot, dry air can raise temperatures fifty degrees in less than an hour. The chinook's fastest heat rise was an amazing forty-four

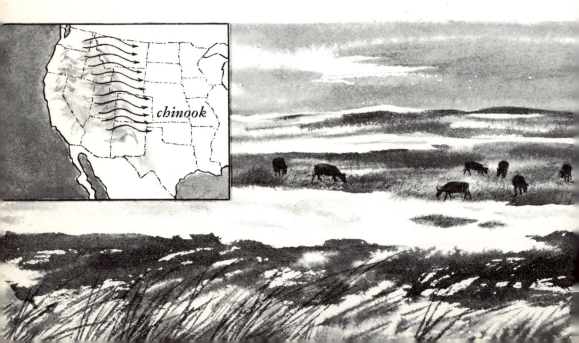

chinook

degrees in fifteen minutes. The Red Indians called this wind the "snoweater," since it can evaporate deep snows even before they have time to melt. Farmers in the region do not have to stock large supplies of feed because the chinook enables cattle to graze off the land several times during midwinter. The chinook's rapid evaporation of deep snows also prevents spring floods.

The chibli of Libya is even hotter than the chinook. Hot air from desert regions is further dried and heated as it crosses the mountains. The scorching chibli has produced the hottest temperature ever recorded on earth—135 degrees at Azizia, Tripolitania, in 1922.

The Santa Ana is a foehn wind of southern California. It blows from the north across the Mojave Desert into the Los Angeles basin. Although it gives the region warm, comfortable winters, this strong, hot, and dry wind also has brought great destruction. During late summer dry spells, when the temperature stays around 100 degrees for days,

fires driven by Santa Ana winds

brush fires break out. Whipped by wind gusts of up to 80 miles per hour in the canyons, the fires may spread with explosive speed across 3000 to 4000 acres an hour. In September, 1970, the Santa Ana burned more than 100,000 acres, destroying many homes and animals. Not surprisingly, the Santa Ana is also called the "devil wind."

A bora, or fall wind, occurs when a mass of cold, high-pressure air that has collected on an interior plateau spills out through a mountain pass. Gravity pulls the heavy air down across lower mountains towards the warmer seashore. The name originally

54

comes from a winter wind that blows southwestward towards the coasts of the Adriatic and the Black Sea in Yugoslavia, Albania, and the Soviet Union.

The mistral of southern France is a famous bora wind that carries very dry, cold air from the north down through the Rhone River valley to the Mediterranean Sea. Williwaws are violent boras that thrust down from steep, snow-covered mountain passes into the narrow fjord waters of Alaska and the Straits of Magellan in southernmost South America. Their unusually sharp descent makes their other name of fall wind very appropriate.

bora, or fall wind

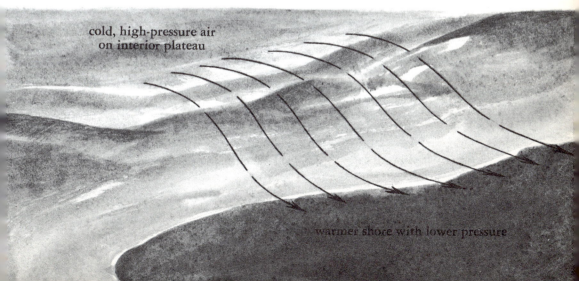

cold, high-pressure air
on interior plateau

warmer shore with lower pressure

Vertical Winds

Jet streams, prevailing winds, daily winds, all are created indirectly by the sun's heat energy. However, there are also smaller, more local, and temporary winds that are powered directly by the sun. Wind not only blows across the earth's surface, it moves up and down. This movement is sometimes known as a vertical wind.

During the day different types of terrain absorb different amounts of the sun's heat. Some areas,

thermals and convection

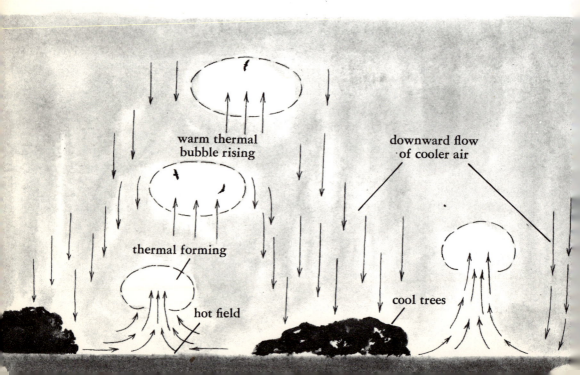

warm thermal
bubble rising

downward flow
of cooler air

thermal forming

hot field

cool trees

such as ploughed fields, rocky hillsides, buildings, motorways, deserts, and beaches, absorb much heat quickly. Other places, like forests, green fields, and bodies of water, heat up more slowly. As air above the hot sections is heated rapidly, it expands and rises. Surrounding cooler air flows towards the lowered pressure created, is heated, and rises in turn. Up and up goes the heated air in a column that finally breaks off in a big ascending bubble.

Rising air currents are called "thermals." Soaring birds like hawks, as well as gliders, use thermal lift to climb high above the earth. Thermals can have a strong effect on local surface winds when they draw air into their centre. In areas surrounding thermals there is a downward return flow of cool air sinking to the surface. This pattern creates an up-and-down circulation called "convection." When convection is especially strong, as on hot summer days, tall, dark-topped thunderclouds may form, accompanied by strong, gusty surface winds.

By day, warmed air rises from valley.

At night, cooled air descends into valley.

Ground fog may form from cooled air.

mountain-valley winds

The sun's daily heating also causes slope, or mountain-valley, winds. The bare slopes of mountains facing the sun heat up more quickly than the level valleys below. During the day warm air rises from the slopes and draws cool air upward from the valleys. At night the high slopes cool quickly, and the cooled air above them drains down into the valleys. This night time drainage leaves large pools of cool air in the valleys. The cooled air often forms ground fog that is cleared away the next morning by the sun's heat.

The same sun, whose heat forces people away from cities and towns, provides power for cooling land-sea winds. In the morning the land, especially a sandy beach, heats up much faster than the ocean. Thermal convection causes warm air to rise over the land. Cool air from the sea is drawn towards lower pressure on land, where it too heats up and rises. Far aloft, the risen air cools and flows out to sea, where it sinks again. All afternoon, as far as thirty miles inland, the sea breeze brings in cooler air.

At night, when the land cools more quickly than the sea, the flow reverses direction. Cool air sinks over land and drains out over the warmer sea. In some countries men fishing from sailing boats take advantage of the early-morning land breeze to reach their fishing grounds. In the afternoon, they return to port with the sea breeze. This daily circulation is the same type as that of the seasonal monsoon.

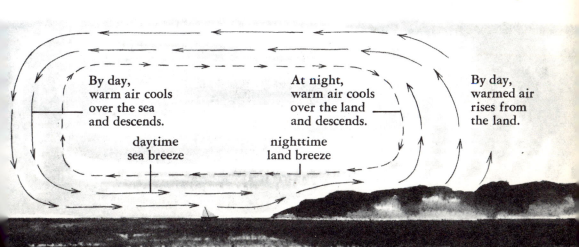

By day, warm air cools over the sea and descends.

At night, warm air cools over the land and descends.

By day, warmed air rises from the land.

daytime sea breeze

nighttime land breeze

Storm Winds

Many winds are the kind we expect and often welcome. Storm winds, on the other hand, are often unexpected and seldom welcome. Winds reach their highest speeds in certain kinds of storms. One is a tropical cyclone, known as a hurricane in the Atlantic Ocean. A cyclone is a large and very low-pressure system, which spirals counterclockwise like other lows. Air descends rapidly at the centre of lowest pressure, forming a calm clear eye about 20 miles wide. In the outer portions moisture is carried upwards to form a sprawling swirl of clouds. Cyclones are about 400 miles wide and move slowly along a curving path with winds up to 200 miles per hour near the centre.

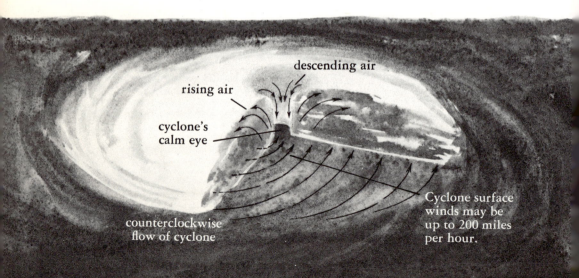

descending air

rising air

cyclone's
calm eye

counterclockwise
flow of cyclone

Cyclone surface
winds may be
up to 200 miles
per hour.

India   East Pakistan   Burma   Bay of Bengal

satellite view of 1970 cyclone in the Bay of Bengal

In the seas of the Far East, cyclones are called typhoons. Many people have been killed by falling buildings, flying debris, as well as the extremely high tides and pounding waves created by the winds of these tremendous storms. In November, 1970, cyclonic winds drove tidal waves over twenty feet high across the crowded low-lying islands in the Bay of Bengal. As many as a million people in East Pakistan (now Bangladesh) may have perished in this storm, which was one of the worst natural disasters on record.

61

The fastest winds of all occur in tornadoes. Sometimes, when a cold front advances against a warm air mass, strong frontal winds aloft override warm air below, preventing it from rising. After the warm air is pushed forward for many miles, it rises suddenly with great force to form a squall line where tornadoes may occur.

A tornado is a funnel-shaped cloud column of tightly spiralling wind with very low pressure at the centre. Advancing swiftly on an unpredictable path beneath darkened skies, it is one of the most terrifying sights in nature. Great destruction occurs where its snaking column touches ground with

tornado

winds that some scientists estimate at over 500 miles per hour. The tornado's centre updraft sucks debris upward with vertical speeds of 100 to 200 miles per hour. Its winds have lifted roofs from large buildings, exploded houses, tossed railway trains from their lines, and have even driven slender pieces of straw into tree trunks. On oceans and large lakes tornadoes suck up water and are called waterspouts.

In other lands storms and their winds have earned names whose very sound gives a feeling of what they are. The willy-willy of Australia, the African simoom, the cordonazo in Mexico, the elephanta of India, and the purga of Siberia are just a few.

Watch the wind signs around you to predict the weather to come. The way trees, columns of smoke, or flags blow indicates both the direction and the speed of the wind. Watch the sky too. Certain types of cloud often occur with particular winds.

63

Try to listen to radio reports direct from the BBC shipping forecasts. They carry much detailed information about winds and the kind of weather they bring. From newspaper and television weather maps, you can learn much about air masses, fronts, storms and their winds. If you want to go farther in the study of winds and weather, there are books that can show you how to build your own simple, inexpensive weather instruments.

The wind is blowing. From a calm, to gentle puffs, to crashing gales, from huge air masses swirling across the world, to a local breeze that barely stirs the grass, the flow of air goes on and on. Weather moves, birds soar, seeds float, boats sail, cities breathe easily or choke in heat and smog. They all depend on the wind.